BUSINESS NEETI : VERSES THAT CAN ENHANCE YOUR BUSINESS

INCLUDED LISTS OF TOOLS YOU CAN USE AND THE LISTS OF VENTURE CAPITALISTS AND ANGEL INVESTORS

ANKIT VASHISHTA

Made with ♥ on the Notion Press Platform
www.notionpress.com

Contents

Contents

Preface

In today's fast-paced and constantly evolving business world, staying ahead of the curve is essential for success. With new technologies emerging every day, it can be challenging for business leaders to keep up and effectively navigate the ever-changing landscape. This book aims to provide guidance and mentorship to CEOs, CMOs, Freelancers, and CTOs in various industries to help them stay ahead of the curve and achieve success in their respective fields.

The book covers a wide range of topics, from Freelancing and Leadership to digital marketing and Handeling Technical Domain. Each chapter is structured with verses inspired by ancient wisdom and formatted to provide concise and actionable insights into the topic at hand. The goal is to provide practical guidance that can be immediately applied in a business context to achieve meaningful results.

This book is not intended to be a comprehensive guide to any one topic, but rather a collection of insights and best practices from experienced industry professionals. By taking a holistic approach to business and technology, readers can gain a better understanding of how different aspects of their organization can work together to achieve success.

I hope that this book will serve as a valuable resource for business leaders looking to stay ahead of the curve in today's ever-changing business landscape. The verses in each chapter are meant to inspire and motivate, while the practical advice offered can help readers take actionable steps toward achieving their goals.

Preface

In today's fast paced and constantly evolving business world, staying ahead of the curve is [illegible] for [illegible]. With new technologies emerging [illegible] [illegible] navigate the ever-changing landscape. [illegible]

[illegible] with verses inspired by [illegible] provide concise and actionable insights into the topic at hand. The goal is to provide practical guidance that can be [illegible] applied in [illegible] business [illegible]

This book is not intended to be a [illegible] guide to any one topic, but rather a [illegible] best practices from experienced industry professionals. By taking a holistic approach to business and technology, readers can gain a better understanding of how different aspects of their organization can work together to achieve success.

I hope that this book will serve as a valuable resource for business leaders looking to stay ahead of the curve in today's ever-changing business landscape. The verses in each chapter are meant to inspire and motivate, while the practical advice offered can help readers take actionable steps toward achieving their goals.

Acknowledgements

Writing this book would not have been possible without the support and encouragement of many people.

First and foremost, I would like to thank all the CEOs, CMOs, Freelancers, and CTOs who have inspired me with their dedication, innovation, and vision. Your commitment to excellence has been a constant source of motivation for me.

I am also deeply grateful to my family and friends for their unwavering support and encouragement throughout this journey. Your love and encouragement have kept me going when the going got tough.

I would like to extend my heartfelt thanks to my publisher and editor for their guidance, expertise, and support. Your tireless efforts have helped me shape this book into what it is today.

Finally, I would like to express my sincere appreciation to all the readers of this book. I hope that the knowledge and insights presented in these pages will be of great value to you as you navigate the ever-evolving landscape of business and technology.

Thank you all for your contributions and support.

CEO Neeti for

Chief Executive Officers (CEOs)

CHAPTER ONE

The Call to Leadership

In the world of business, the journey of a CEO is long and arduous. As you step into this role, you must be ready to face challenges and make difficult decisions. Like Arjuna on the battlefield, you must be prepared to confront the forces that threaten the success of your organization. This chapter sets the stage for your journey, calling on you to be a leader who is both courageous and wise.

Verse 1:

As the CEO, you stand at the helm,
Guiding your organization to its destiny.
Like a charioteer on the battlefield,
You must steer your company through challenges aplenty.

Verse 2:

The world of business is a battleground,
Where the strong and the strategic survive.
To emerge victorious, you must be resolute,
With a clear vision and a sharp mind.

Verse 3:

As Arjuna faced his foes with trepidation,
So too must you confront the challenges ahead.
But fear not, for with courage and conviction,
You will overcome all obstacles, alive and well-fed.

Verse 4:
Be mindful of your thoughts and your actions,
For they shape the destiny of your enterprise.
Make decisions that are wise and just,
And success will surely materialize.
Verse 5:
Remember that you are not alone,
For there are those who look up to you.
Be a leader that inspires and motivates,
And your team will follow you through and through.
Verse 6:
So heed this call to leadership,
And rise to the challenge at hand.
With perseverance and determination,
You will lead your company to greatness, grand.
Verse 7:
In the world of business, there are no guarantees,
Success is earned through hard work and dedication.
So be steadfast in your pursuit of excellence,
And let your passion drive your organization.
Verse 8:
Be mindful of the risks and the rewards,
And make decisions with a balanced mind.
For every opportunity, there is a cost,
And every loss can be a lesson, refined.
Verse 9:
Like a general on the battlefield,
You must be strategic and tactical.
Anticipate your rivals' moves and stay ahead,
And let your foresight be your guide, magical.
Verse 10:
Be a visionary, a dreamer, and a doer,
And let your creativity run free.

For in the realm of business, innovation rules,
And those who dare to dream, they succeed, truly.
Verse 11:
Be a leader who leads by example,
With integrity and honor in all you do.
Let your actions be your words,
And your character, a shining virtue.
Verse 12:
Stay grounded in your values and principles,
And let them guide you through thick and thin.
For a CEO without a moral compass,
Is destined to fail, amidst all the din.
Verse 13:
Surround yourself with the best and the brightest,
And let their talents complement your own.
Together you can achieve great things,
And create a culture of excellence, sown.
Verse 14:
Be empathetic to your employees' needs,
For they are the lifeblood of your organization.
Treat them with respect and compassion,
And watch them flourish, with a renewed motivation.
Verse 15:
In the world of business, there are no shortcuts,
Success is earned through hard work and grit.
So be persistent, patient, and resilient,
And let your determination be your anchor, fit.
Verse 16:
Be aware of the changing landscape,
And adapt to the times with agility.
For in the face of disruption and innovation,
Only those who adapt survive, with ingenuity.
Verse 17:

Be mindful of the impact of your decisions,
On the environment, society, and the economy.
For a CEO who is socially responsible,
Is one who earns the trust of the community.
Verse 18:
Be a lifelong learner, and stay curious,
For knowledge is power, and wisdom, priceless.
Invest in your own growth and development,
And let your expertise be your greatest asset, wireless.
Verse 19:
Be humble in your successes,
And gracious in your failures, too.
For a CEO who can learn from both,
Is one who can lead his organization anew.
Verse 20:
In the end, the journey of a CEO,
Is not just about success and wealth.
It's about leaving a legacy that inspires,
And creating a future that's bright, stealth.

CHAPTER TWO

The Path of Strategy

As a CEO, your ability to formulate and execute strategy is critical to the success of your organization. In this chapter, we explore the path of strategy, drawing on the timeless wisdom of the Bhagavad Gita to guide you in your quest for success.

Verse 1:
To win the battle of business, you must have a plan,
A strategy that's clear and concise.
It must be flexible, yet focused,
And it must be executed with precision, wise.
Verse 2:
Like Arjuna, you must survey the battlefield,
And assess your strengths and weaknesses.
You must understand your competition,
And anticipate their moves, with shrewdness.
Verse 3:
Formulate your strategy with care,
And let it be guided by your purpose and vision.
Be mindful of your resources and capabilities,
And create a plan that leads to precision.
Verse 4:
Set clear goals and objectives,
And break them down into actionable steps.

Measure your progress, and adjust your course,
With agility and foresight, a business adept.
Verse 5:
Be mindful of the risks and uncertainties,
And have contingency plans in place.
For in the world of business, anything can happen,
And only those who are prepared can face, with grace.
Verse 6:
Be mindful of the long-term view,
And let your strategy be sustainable.
Be conscious of the impact of your actions,
On the environment, society, and the global stable.
Verse 7:
In the realm of business, there are no absolutes,
And no strategy can guarantee success.
So be prepared to experiment and learn,
And let your failures be a lesson, with finesse.
Verse 8:
Be open to new ideas and perspectives,
And let innovation be your guiding light.
For those who can adapt and evolve,
Are those who can survive, with might.
Verse 9:
Stay focused on your core competencies,
And let them be the foundation of your strategy.
For a CEO who knows what he does best,
Is one who can lead his organization to destiny.
Verse 10:
Be mindful of your customers' needs,
And let them be the center of your strategy.
For a CEO who can meet their demands,
Is one who can create a loyal community, with synergy.
Verse 11:

In the end, the path of strategy,
Is one that requires vision and skill.
But with determination and wisdom,
You can lead your organization, to fulfill.
Verse 12:
As a CEO, you must think long-term,
And plan for the future, with care.
Don't be swayed by short-term gains,
But aim for sustained growth, rare.
Verse 13:
Be mindful of the changing landscape,
And adapt your strategy, with grace.
For those who can stay ahead of the curve,
Are those who can thrive, in any space.
Verse 14:
Be cautious of the pitfalls of success,
And guard against complacency and pride.
For those who rest on their laurels,
Are those who will fall, with no stride.
Verse 15:
Be strategic in your investments,
And let them align with your goals.
Don't be swayed by fads and trends,
But invest in what truly rolls.
Verse 16:
Be mindful of your financial health,
And let your strategy reflect your fiscal reality.
For a CEO who can manage his finances,
Is one who can lead his organization, with clarity.
Verse 17:
Be aware of the power of collaboration,
And let it be part of your strategy.
For those who can forge partnerships,

Are those who can create value, with synergy.

Verse 18:

Be innovative in your marketing,
And let it reflect your unique value proposition.
For a CEO who can tell his story,
Is one who can capture his audience's attention, with no opposition.

Verse 19:

Be transparent in your communication,
And let it be part of your strategy, true.
For those who can build trust with stakeholders,
Are those who can create a strong brand, anew.

Verse 20:

In the end, the path of strategy,
Is one that requires foresight and agility.
But with perseverance and a clear vision,
You can lead your organization, to its destiny.

Verse 21:

Be mindful of your organizational culture,
And let it reflect your strategy, with clarity.
For a CEO who can cultivate a strong culture,
Is one who can inspire his team, with solidarity.

Verse 22:

Be proactive in your risk management,
And let it be an integral part of your strategy.
For those who can mitigate risks effectively,
Are those who can ensure business continuity, with efficacy.

Verse 23:

Be strategic in your resource allocation,
And let it be based on data-driven insights.
For a CEO who can allocate resources effectively,
Is one who can optimize his organization's might.

Verse 24:
Be mindful of your competitive advantage,
And let it be the driving force of your strategy.
For those who can leverage their advantages,
Are those who can outperform their competitors, with agility.
Verse 25:
Be mindful of the impact of technology,
And let it be part of your strategy, with foresight.
For a CEO who can embrace technology,
Is one who can create a competitive edge, with insight.
Verse 26:
Be strategic in your talent management,
And let it be the cornerstone of your strategy.
For those who can attract and retain top talent,
Are those who can build a high-performance team, with acuity.
Verse 27:
Be mindful of your social responsibility,
And let it be part of your strategy, with empathy.
For a CEO who can be socially responsible,
Is one who can earn the trust and loyalty of his community.
Verse 28:
Be strategic in your customer engagement,
And let it be based on a deep understanding of their needs.
For those who can engage their customers effectively,
Are those who can create a loyal customer base, with leads.
Verse 29:
Be mindful of your industry trends,
And let them inform your strategy, with foresight.

For a CEO who can stay ahead of industry trends,
Is one who can create a sustainable business, with right.
Verse 30:
In the end, the path of strategy,
Is one that requires courage and vision.
But with a clear sense of purpose and direction,
You can lead your organization, to its ultimate mission.

CHAPTER THREE

The Art of Execution

Verse 1:

Strategy without execution is merely a dream,
To make it a reality, execution is the key.
As a CEO, you must master the art of execution,
To turn your vision into a tangible reality.
Verse 2:
Execution is the bridge between strategy and results,
And it requires a disciplined and focused approach.
As a CEO, you must lead your team through execution,
And ensure that everyone is aligned and on track.
Verse 3:
Execution is not about doing things right,
But it is about doing the right things, with might.
As a CEO, you must prioritize and focus,
On the most critical initiatives, with insight.
Verse 4:
Execution requires a sense of urgency,
And a commitment to timely delivery.
As a CEO, you must set clear timelines and milestones,
And hold your team accountable for their delivery.
Verse 5:
Execution requires a willingness to learn,
And a flexibility to adapt and adjust.

As a CEO, you must foster a culture of continuous improvement,

And encourage your team to experiment and adjust.

Verse 6:

Execution requires attention to detail,

And a focus on the little things that matter.

As a CEO, you must ensure that nothing falls through the cracks,

And that every detail is taken care of, with chatter.

Verse 7:

Execution requires effective communication,

And a clarity of roles and responsibilities.

As a CEO, you must ensure that everyone knows their part,

And that communication flows freely and respectfully.

Verse 8:

Execution requires a sense of ownership,

And a commitment to excellence and quality.

As a CEO, you must empower your team to take ownership,

And encourage them to strive for excellence, with ability.

Verse 9:

Execution requires a strong sense of teamwork,

And a willingness to collaborate and cooperate.

As a CEO, you must foster a culture of teamwork and collaboration,

And encourage your team to work together, with mate.

Verse 10:

Execution requires a focus on outcomes,

And a willingness to measure and track.

As a CEO, you must define clear metrics and KPIs,

And use them to monitor progress and stay on track.

Verse 11:
In the end, the art of execution,
Is what separates successful organizations, from the rest.
As a CEO, you must master this art,
To ensure that your organization can be the best.

CHAPTER FOUR

The Power of Leadership

Verse 1:

Leadership is the cornerstone of success,
And it requires a deep understanding of human behavior.
As a CEO, you must master the art of leadership,
To inspire and guide your team, with fervor.
Verse 2:
Leadership is not about position or authority,
But it is about influence and inspiration.
As a CEO, you must lead by example,
And inspire your team to action, with motivation.
Verse 3:
Leadership requires a clear sense of purpose,
And a vision that inspires and motivates.
As a CEO, you must define a compelling purpose,
And communicate it to your team, with grace.
Verse 4:
Leadership requires a willingness to listen,
And a humility to learn from others.
As a CEO, you must listen to your team's input,
And be open to new ideas and perspectives, with covers.

Verse 5:

Leadership requires empathy and compassion,
And a deep understanding of your team's needs.
As a CEO, you must care about your team's well-being,
And support them in their personal and professional leads.

Verse 6:

Leadership requires courage and conviction,
And a willingness to take calculated risks.
As a CEO, you must be bold and decisive,
And have the courage to make tough decisions, with tricks.

Verse 7:

Leadership requires authenticity and integrity,
And a commitment to doing the right thing.
As a CEO, you must lead with honesty and transparency,
And earn the trust and respect of your team, with wing.

Verse 8:

Leadership requires a focus on results,
And a commitment to achieving your goals.
As a CEO, you must set clear expectations and goals,
And hold yourself and your team accountable, with scrolls.

Verse 9:

Leadership requires a willingness to learn and grow,
And a commitment to continuous improvement.
As a CEO, you must seek out feedback and learning,
And constantly improve your leadership skills, with movement.

Verse 10:

Leadership is not a one-time event,
But it is a continuous journey of growth and development.

As a CEO, you must commit to lifelong learning,
And constantly evolve and adapt, with fulfilment.
Verse 11:
In the end, the power of leadership,
Is what separates great CEOs, from the rest.
As a CEO, you must embrace the power of leadership,
To inspire and guide your team, to their best.

CHAPTER FIVE

The Importance of Culture

Verse 1:

Culture is the DNA of an organization,
And it determines how it behaves and operates.
As a CEO, you must understand the importance of culture,
And shape it in a way that aligns with your vision and mandates.

Verse 2:

Culture is not just a set of values and norms,
But it is a way of being and doing things.
As a CEO, you must lead by example,
And embody the culture you want to see in your settings.

Verse 3:

Culture can be a powerful force for good,
Or it can be a destructive force for ill.
As a CEO, you must create a positive culture,
That fosters collaboration, innovation and goodwill.

Verse 4:

Culture requires a deep sense of purpose,
And a commitment to shared values and vision.

As a CEO, you must define a clear purpose and values,
And communicate them consistently and with precision.

Verse 5:
Culture requires inclusivity and diversity,
And a willingness to embrace different perspectives.
As a CEO, you must create a culture of openness,
That values and respects all voices, with objectives.

Verse 6:
Culture requires a focus on employee well-being,
And a commitment to work-life balance.
As a CEO, you must create a culture of care,
That supports and empowers employees to enhance.

Verse 7:
Culture requires a focus on continuous learning,
And a willingness to embrace change and innovation.
As a CEO, you must foster a culture of learning,
That encourages experimentation and exploration.

Verse 8:
Culture requires a focus on ethics and integrity,
And a commitment to doing the right thing.
As a CEO, you must ensure that your culture,
Values honesty, transparency and ethical string.

Verse 9:
Culture requires a focus on customer satisfaction,
And a commitment to delivering value.
As a CEO, you must create a culture of customer-centricity,
That puts the needs of your customers first, with ability.

Verse 10:
In the end, culture is the heart and soul,
Of an organization's success and sustainability.
As a CEO, you must prioritize culture,

And nurture it with care and responsibility, with agility.
Verse 11:
By embracing the importance of culture,
You can create an organization that thrives.
As a CEO, you must commit to building a strong culture,
That inspires and motivates, and truly drives.

CHAPTER SIX

The Importance of Innovation

Verse 1:

Innovation is the key to long-term success,
And it requires a willingness to embrace change.
As a CEO, you must understand the importance of innovation,
And create an environment that fosters it, with range.

Verse 2:

Innovation is not just about creating new products,
But it is about finding new ways to solve problems.
As a CEO, you must encourage your team to think creatively,
And empower them to take risks and become more awesome.

Verse 3:

Innovation requires a deep understanding of customer needs,
And a commitment to delivering value.
As a CEO, you must foster a culture of customer-centricity,
And encourage your team to listen and learn from them, with agility.

Verse 4:

Innovation requires a focus on collaboration,

And a willingness to embrace diverse perspectives.

As a CEO, you must create a culture of openness and inclusivity,

That encourages teamwork and supports collective objectives.

Verse 5:

Innovation requires a focus on experimentation,

And a willingness to learn from failure.

As a CEO, you must create a culture of learning and growth,

That values experimentation and supports continuous learning for sure.

Verse 6:

Innovation requires a focus on technology,

And a commitment to staying ahead of the curve.

As a CEO, you must embrace digital transformation,

And invest in the technology that enables innovation to preserve.

Verse 7:

Innovation requires a focus on agility,

And a willingness to adapt to changing markets.

As a CEO, you must create a culture of flexibility,

That enables your organization to respond to shifts and impacts.

Verse 8:

Innovation requires a focus on leadership,

And a willingness to inspire and motivate.

As a CEO, you must lead by example,

And encourage your team to take risks and innovate, with great.

Verse 9:

Innovation requires a focus on strategy,
And a commitment to long-term vision.
As a CEO, you must create a culture of innovation,
That aligns with your overall strategic ambition.

Verse 10:

In the end, innovation is the lifeblood of growth,
And it enables organizations to stay ahead of the pack.
As a CEO, you must embrace the importance of innovation,
And create an environment that enables your team to attack.

Verse 11:

By embracing the importance of innovation,
You can create an organization that thrives.
As a CEO, you must commit to fostering innovation,
And empower your team to push the boundaries and arrive.

CHAPTER SEVEN

Fostering Corporate Social Responsibility

Verse 1:

Corporate Social Responsibility, or CSR,

Is a commitment to doing business ethically and responsibly.

As a CEO, you must understand the importance of CSR,

And create a culture that values sustainability and accountability.

Verse 2:

CSR requires a focus on social and environmental impact,

And a commitment to creating positive change.

As a CEO, you must prioritize the triple bottom line,

And ensure that your organization operates in a sustainable range.

Verse 3:

CSR requires a focus on stakeholder engagement,

And a commitment to transparency and ethical governance.

As a CEO, you must communicate openly with stakeholders,

And ensure that your business practices are ethical and beyond reproach.

Verse 4:

CSR requires a focus on employee well-being,

And a commitment to creating a positive workplace culture.

As a CEO, you must prioritize the health and safety of your employees,

And create a culture that supports work-life balance and nurtures.

Verse 5:

CSR requires a focus on community engagement,

And a commitment to giving back to society.

As a CEO, you must prioritize community outreach,

And support initiatives that make a positive impact on humanity.

Verse 6:

CSR requires a focus on responsible supply chain management,

And a commitment to ethical sourcing and manufacturing.

As a CEO, you must ensure that your suppliers and vendors,

Adhere to ethical and sustainable practices, with purposeful creating.

Verse 7:

CSR requires a focus on diversity and inclusion,

And a commitment to creating a culture of respect and equity.

As a CEO, you must ensure that your organization values diversity,

And creates an inclusive workplace that supports the full spectrum of humanity.

Verse 8:

CSR requires a focus on ethical financial practices,

And a commitment to avoiding corruption and bribery.

As a CEO, you must ensure that your organization operates with integrity,

And prioritizes ethical financial practices that ensure long-term stability.

Verse 9:

CSR requires a focus on innovation and sustainability,

And a commitment to reducing your organization's environmental impact.

As a CEO, you must prioritize sustainability initiatives,

And encourage your team to think creatively about reducing waste and enhancing natural ecosystems in fact.

Verse 10:

In the end, CSR is not just a business practice,

But it is a moral imperative for organizations today.

As a CEO, you must embrace the importance of CSR,

And commit to doing business ethically and responsibly, as a way.

Verse 11:

By embracing CSR and creating a culture of sustainability,

You can create an organization that makes a positive impact.

As a CEO, you must prioritize CSR initiatives,

And ensure that your business practices align with your moral compass, with tact.

CHAPTER EIGHT

Fostering Finance

Verse 1:

Finance is the lifeblood of any business,
And as a CEO, you must have a deep understanding of it.
It is essential to manage your finances wisely,
To ensure that your business stays healthy and fit.

Verse 2:

Financial planning is crucial for success,
As it helps to ensure the long-term viability of your business.
It involves setting goals and creating budgets,
And making strategic decisions that are both sound and cautious.

Verse 3:

Cash flow management is an essential skill,
And one that every CEO must master.
You must ensure that your business has enough liquidity,
To meet its financial obligations and avoid disaster.

Verse 4:

Profit and loss management is also critical,
As it helps to track the financial health of your business.
You must monitor your revenue and expenses closely,
To ensure that your profits stay positive and auspicious.

Verse 5:

Managing debt and financing is also important,

As it helps to ensure that your business has the capital it needs.

You must be strategic about taking on debt or raising capital,

And make decisions that will help your business grow and succeed.

Verse 6:

Managing investments and assets is another skill,

That every CEO must develop over time.

You must ensure that your business's assets are optimized,

And that you invest in areas that will help your business climb.

Verse 7:

Risk management is a critical part of finance,

And it involves identifying and mitigating potential risks.

You must create a plan to address risks and emergencies,

To ensure that your business stays healthy and brisk.

Verse 8:

Financial reporting is essential for transparency,

And it helps to ensure that your business is accountable.

You must ensure that your financial statements are accurate,

And that you communicate clearly with stakeholders who are reliable.

Verse 9:

Financial governance is also important,

And it involves creating policies that govern financial decision-making.

You must ensure that your financial policies align with your values,

And that you create a culture of transparency that is both open and fair.

Verse 10:

Ultimately, finance is a critical component of your business,

And it requires your attention and focus every day.

As a CEO, you must foster a strong financial culture,

And ensure that your business is financially sound and okay.

Verse 11:

By focusing on finance and making strategic decisions,

You can create a business that is financially strong and stable.

As a CEO, you must prioritize finance initiatives,

And ensure that your business is equipped to face any challenge, and able.

CHAPTER NINE

Funding

Verse 1:

Funding is the lifeblood of any growing business,

And as a CEO, you must be well-versed in the art of securing funds.

There are many different sources of funding available,

And it's important to find the right one that suits your business and funds.

Verse 2:

Investment is one of the most common ways to secure funding,

And it can come from a variety of sources, including venture capitalists and angel investors.

To attract investors, you must have a clear and compelling business plan,

And a thorough understanding of your market and competition for investors.

Verse 3:

Crowdfunding is another popular way to raise funds,

And it involves soliciting funds from a large number of individuals online.

To be successful in crowdfunding, you must have a clear message and pitch,

And offer compelling rewards or equity in your business to backers who are supportive.

Verse 4:

Bank loans and lines of credit are traditional sources of funding,

And they can provide access to significant amounts of capital for your business.

To secure a loan, you must have a strong credit history and a well-established business,

And demonstrate a clear plan for repayment that is both feasible and reliable.

Verse 5:

Government grants and incentives are also a potential source of funding,

And they can provide funding for research and development, job creation, and more.

To be eligible for government funding, you must meet certain criteria and apply,

And demonstrate how your business will benefit from the funding and why you deserve to comply.

Verse 6:

Corporate partnerships and strategic alliances can also provide funding,

And they can offer access to resources and expertise that can help your business grow.

To secure a partnership or alliance, you must demonstrate the value of your business,

And show how your partnership will benefit both your business and the partner's business as well.

Verse 7:

Bootstrapping is a common way to start a business,

And it involves using personal savings or resources.

It can be an effective way to get started,

But may not provide the necessary growth and courses.

Verse 8:

Debt financing is another option to consider,

And it involves borrowing money from lenders.

It can provide flexible terms and lower costs,

But may also increase financial risk and stir-up contenders.

Verse 9:

Regardless of the funding option you choose,

You must be strategic and cautious in your approach.

You must ensure that the terms are fair and reasonable,

And that the funding aligns with your business's goals and reproach.

Verse 10:

You must also be prepared to manage the funding effectively,

And use it in a way that helps your business grow and thrive.

You must be accountable for the funds you receive,

And ensure that they are used in the most productive drive.

Verse 11:

Finally, funding is just one part of the equation,

And as a CEO, you must also focus on generating revenue.

You must create a business model that is sustainable,

And ensure that your business can generate profits that are stable.

Verse 12:

By being strategic about funding and focusing on revenue,

You can create a business that is financially stable and successful.

As a CEO, you must be willing to make difficult decisions,

And ensure that your business is equipped to handle any test or trial.

CHAPTER TEN

List of Venture Capitalists and Angel Investors with Websites in India State-wise

(Note: List is comprehensive and subject to change)

List of Investors in India

- *Andhra Pradesh*

1. Endiya Partners
2. Parampara Capital
3. 50K Ventures
4. Anthill Ventures

5. AWE Funds

- ### *Bihar*

1. Indian Angel Network
2. Omidyar Network India Advisors

- ### *Chandigarh*

1. Indian Angel Network

- ### *Chhattisgarh*

1. 36 Inc

- ### *Delhi*

1. Indian Angel Network
2. LetsVenture
3. Blume Ventures
4. Nexus Venture Partners
5. SAIF Partners

-

Gujarat

1. GVFL
2. Infuse Ventures
3. Venture Catalysts
4. Unicorn India Ventures

•

Haryana

1. Blume Ventures
2. Nexus Venture Partners
3. Kae Capital
4. Indian Angel Network
5. 500 Startups
6. Axilor Ventures
7. SAIF Partners
8. Accel Partners
9. Helion Venture Partners
10. Matrix Partners

•

Karnataka

1. Accel Partners
2. Sequoia Capital
3. Nexus Venture Partners
4. Kalaari Capital
5. SAIF Partners
6. IDG Ventures India

7. Blume Ventures
8. Omidyar Network India Advisors
9. Chiratae Ventures (formerly IDG Ventures India)
10. Inventus Capital Partners
11. Helion Venture Partners
12. Axilor Ventures
13. 3one4 Capital
14. Stellaris Venture Partners
15. India Quotient
16. Unicorn India Ventures
17. Jungle Ventures
18. Endiya Partners
19. Lightspeed India Partners
20. Intel Capital
21. Norwest Venture Partners
22. Elevation Capital (formerly SAIF Partners)
23. Bharat Innovation Fund
24. IAN Fund
25. Prime Venture Partners
26. Artha Venture Fund
27. Better Capital
28. Unitus Ventures
29. 500 Startups
30. Fidelity Investments
31. Fosun RZ Capital
32. Gaja Capital
33. IvyCap Ventures
34. Naspers Ventures
35. Pi Ventures
36. Qualcomm Ventures
37. SRI Capital
38. Trifecta Capital
39. Ventureast

40. YourNest Venture Capital
41. Exfinity Venture Partners
42. India Angel Network
43. Mumbai Angels Network
44. Hyderabad Angels
45. LetsVenture
46. KStart Capital
47. StartupXseed Ventures
48. Menterra Venture Advisors
49. Aavishkaar Venture Management
50. Ankur Capital Fund

- ***Kerala***

1. Indian Angel Network (IAN)
2. Seedfund
3. Kerala Venture Capital Fund (KVCF)
4. Accel Partners
5. Inventus Capital Partners
6. Blume Ventures
7. Nexus Venture Partners
8. SAIF Partners
9. Helion Venture Partners
10. IDG Ventures India
11. Endiya Partners
12. Axilor Ventures
13. Artha Venture Fund
14. Ankur Capital
15. Unitus Seed Fund
16. AngelList
17. 3one4 Capital

18. Ideaspring Capital
19. Unicorn India Ventures
20. LetsVenture
21. YourNest
22. WaterBridge Ventures
23. Orios Venture Partners
24. Kae Capital
25. Aspada Investment Advisors
26. Ventureast
27. Exfinity Venture Partners
28. pi Ventures
29. Better Capital
30. Stellaris Venture Partners.

- ### *Maharastra*

1. Blume Ventures
2. Sequoia Capital India
3. Nexus Venture Partners
4. Kae Capital
5. Accel Partners
6. SAIF Partners
7. IDG Ventures India
8. Matrix Partners India
9. Orios Venture Partners
10. Indian Angel Network (IAN)
11. LetsVenture
12. Mumbai Angels Network
13. Unicorn India Ventures
14. Kalaari Capital
15. Chiratae Ventures (formerly IDG Ventures India)

16. Lightbox Ventures
17. 100X.VC
18. KStart Capital
19. Global Innovation Fund (GIF)
20. Fireside Ventures.

-

Punjab

1. Accel Partners
2. Sequoia Capital India
3. Nexus Venture Partners
4. Saama Capital
5. Matrix Partners India
6. Orios Venture Partners
7. Stellaris Venture Partners
8. Kae Capital
9. IDG Ventures India
10. Inventus Capital Partners
11. 3one4 Capital
12. Blume Ventures
13. Axilor Ventures
14. Bharat Innovation Fund
15. IvyCap Ventures
16. Endiya Partners
17. WaterBridge Ventures
18. Unicorn India Ventures
19. Indian Angel Network
20. LetsVenture

-

Rajasthan

1. Rajasthan Venture Capital Fund
2. Artha Venture Fund
3. Blume Ventures
4. YourNest Venture Capital
5. AngelList India
6. Omnivore
7. Nexus Venture Partners
8. Seedfund
9. Accel Partners
10. SAIF Partners
11. 3one4 Capital
12. Stellaris Venture Partners
13. Kalaari Capital
14. India Quotient
15. Matrix Partners India
16. Chiratae Ventures (formerly IDG Ventures India)
17. Bharat Innovation Fund
18. WaterBridge Ventures
19. Iron Pillar
20. Sequoia Capital India

•

Tamil Nadu

1. Accel Partners
2. IDG Ventures India
3. Kalaari Capital
4. IvyCap Ventures
5. Pi Ventures

6. Inventus Capital
7. Unitus Seed Fund
8. Exfinity Venture Partners
9. Endiya Partners
10. Ideaspring Capital
11. Artha Venture Fund
12. YourNest Venture Capital
13. Axilor Ventures
14. Unicorn India Ventures
15. 3one4 Capital
16. Speciale Invest
17. Bharat Innovation Fund
18. Omnivore Partners
19. CIIE.CO
20. Ventureast.

-

Telangana

1. 50K Ventures
2. AdvantEdge Partners
3. Anthill Ventures
4. Hyderabad Angels
5. Indian Angel Network
6. Kalaari Capital
7. LetsVenture
8. Pi Ventures
9. Unicorn India Ventures
10. Ventureast

-

Uttar Pradesh

1. Ankur Capital
2. SRI Capital
3. Unicorn India Ventures
4. Indian Angel Network
5. 3one4 Capital

•

Uttrakhand

1. Swan Angel Network
2. Uttarakhand Angels Network

•

West Bengal

1. Sequoia Capital India
2. Accel Partners
3. SAIF Partners
4. Chiratae Ventures (formerly IDG)
5. Indian Angel Network

Additionally go to https://www.ivca.in/membership for more

List of Investors in USA

1. New Capital Partners

2. No venture capital firms found
3. Canal Partners
4. Grayhawk Capital
5. Tallwave Capital
6. Fund for Arkansas' Future
7. Sequoia Capital
8. Andreessen Horowitz
9. Accel Partners
10. Greylock Partners
11. Kleiner Perkins
12. Lightspeed Venture Partners
13. Bessemer Venture Partners
14. Benchmark
15. Founders Fund
16. Mayfield Fund
17. Menlo Ventures
18. NEA
19. Battery Ventures
20. Index Ventures
21. IVP
22. Redpoint Ventures
23. First Round Capital
24. 500 Startups
25. Y Combinator
26. Plug and Play Tech Center
27. Sapphire Ventures
28. True Ventures
29. WestRiver Group
30. Foundry Group
31. Access Venture Partners
32. Grotech Ventures
33. Next Frontier Capital
34. High Country Venture

35. Connecticut Innovations
36. No venture capital firms found
37. H.I.G. Capital
38. New World Angels
39. Capital Factory
40. BIP Capital
41. Tech Square Ventures
42. Noro-Moseley Partners
43. Sultan Ventures
44. No venture capital firms found
45. Pritzker Group Venture Capital
46. Chicago Ventures
47. Cultivian Sandbox Ventures
48. Elevate Ventures
49. Next Level Ventures
50. Flyover Capital
51. Access Ventures
52. No venture capital firms found
53. No venture capital firms found
54. Camden Partners
55. Revolution Ventures
56. New Enterprise Associates
57. General Catalyst
58. F-Prime Capital
59. Spark Capital
60. Matrix Partners
61. Bessemer Venture Partners
62. Flagship Pioneering
63. Accomplice
64. Polaris Partners
65. Detroit Venture Partners
66. Grand Ventures
67. Arboretum Ventures

68. Brightstone Venture Capital
69. Arthur Ventures
70. No venture capital firms found
71. Cultivation Capital
72. Lewis & Clark Ventures
73. Next Frontier Capital
74. Dundee Venture Capital
75. No venture capital firms found
76. Borealis Ventures
77. Edison Partners
78. Tech Council Ventures
79. Newark Venture Partners
80. Insight Partners
81. Jump Capital
82. Osage Venture Partners
83. Cottonwood Technology Fund
84. Union Square Ventures
85. First Round Capital
86. Brooklyn Bridge Ventures
87. RRE Ventures
88. ff Venture Capital
89. Greycroft Partners
90. Lerer Hippeau
91. Primary Venture Partners
92. Two Sigma Ventures
93. Bull City Venture Partners
94. IDEA Fund Partners
95. No venture capital firms found
96. Drive Capital
97. Rev1 Ventures
98. NCT Ventures
99. i2E
100. Elevate Capital

101. Voyager Capital
102. FirstMark Capital
103. 1315 Capital
104. Ben Franklin Technology Partners
105. No venture capital firms found
106. VentureSouth
107. SC Launch
108. No venture capital firms found
109. FCA Venture Partners
110. Innova Memphis
111. S3 Ventures
112. Mercury Fund
113. Austin Ventures
114. LiveOak Venture Partners
115. Silverton Partners
116. Techstars
117. BIP Capital
118. Sevin Rosen Funds
119. Next Coast Ventures
120. True Wealth Ventures
121. Signal Peak Ventures
122. Kickstart Seed Fund
123. Pelion Venture Partners
124. FreshTracks Capital
125. New Enterprise Associates (NEA)
126. Revolution
127. QED Investors
128. CIT GAP Funds
129. Valhalla Partners
130. Madrona Venture Group
131. Voyager Capital
132. Trilogy Equity Partners
133. Ignition Partners

134. No venture capital firms found
135. Wisconsin Investment Partners
136. Venture Investors
137. HealthX Ventures

List of Investors in UK

1. Albion Capital Group LLP
2. Amadeus Capital Partners
3. Atomico
4. Beringea
5. Draper Esprit
6. Episode 1
7. Frog Capital
8. Forward Partners
9. Index Ventures
10. MMC Ventures
11. Notion Capital
12. Octopus Ventures
13. Passion Capital
14. Pembroke VCT
15. Seedcamp
16. Seraphim Capital
17. Sussex Place Ventures
18. Touchstone Innovations
19. White Star Capital
20. 24Haymarket
21. Accel
22. Advent Life Sciences
23. AlbionVC
24. Anthemis

25. AlbionVC
26. Amadeus Capital Partners
27. Atomico
28. Augmentum Fintech
29. BGF
30. Blenheim Chalcot
31. Bridges Fund Management
32. Balderton Capital
33. Beacon Capital
34. Beringea
35. BGF
36. Blockchain Capital Partners
37. Blossom Capital
38. Connect Ventures
39. Conduit Ventures
40. Dawn Capital
41. Downing Ventures
42. Draper Esprit
43. Episode 1 Ventures
44. Felix Capital
45. Firstminute Capital
46. Forward Partners
47. Fuel Ventures
48. Grafton Capital
49. Hambro Perks
50. Hoxton Ventures
51. Index Ventures
52. InMotion Ventures
53. Insight Partners
54. IQ Capital Partners
55. Kindred Capital
56. Kreos Capital
57. LocalGlobe

58. Mosaic Ventures
59. Notion Capital
60. Octopus Ventures
61. Passion Capital
62. Pembroke VCT
63. Playground Global
64. QVentures
65. MMC Ventures
66. Moonfire
67. Mosaic Ventures
68. Mustard Seed
69. Nauta Capital
70. New Wave Ventures
71. Notion Capital
72. Octopus Ventures
73. Oxford Capital Partners
74. Oxford Sciences Innovation
75. Palatine Private Equity
76. Passion Capital
77. Pembroke VCT
78. Playfair Capital
79. Playground Global
80. Praetura Ventures
81. QVentures
82. Rakuten Capital
83. Redalpine
84. Rianta Capital
85. Rocket Internet
86. Saïd Business School
87. Scottish Equity Partners
88. Seedcamp
89. Seraphim Capital
90. Seedrs

91. Seedrs
92. Seedrs EIS
93. Seedrs Secondary Market
94. Silicon Valley Bank
95. Smedvig Capital
96. SoftBank Group Corp.
97. Speedinvest
98. Speedinvest x
99. Startup Funding Club
100. Station12
101. Stride VC

Freelance Neeti for

Freelancers

CHAPTER ELEVEN

The Path of the Freelancer

Verse 1:

"Arise, O freelancer, and embrace your work,
With a focused mind and spirit unshook,
Let not the distractions of the world take hold,
Stay steadfast on your path, be strong and bold."

Verse 2:

In the art of freelancing, skill is key,
Hone your craft, and learn continually,
Sharpen your expertise, and never stop,
Your knowledge is the foundation of your crop.

Verse 3:

To succeed in this path, passion is a must,
Love what you do, and in it, put your trust,
For when you work from your heart and soul,
Your efforts will yield a bountiful goal.

Verse 4:

As a freelancer, you're your own guide,
Take ownership of your work, and strive,
To be your best, and exceed expectation,
Success will follow, with determination.

Verse 5:

In the world of freelancing, one must adapt,
To the changing trends, and stay on track,
Embrace innovation, and be flexible,
To stay ahead and be unbeatable.
Verse 6:
Communication is key, in all that you do,
Listen to your clients, and their needs pursue,
Be clear in your message, and responsive too,
For a good reputation, this is all true.
Verse 7:
As you embark on this journey alone,
Remember, you're part of a bigger zone,
Connect with others, learn from their stories,
And grow together, in all your glories.
Verse 8:
In the face of challenges, stay composed,
The key is resilience, don't be opposed,
To failure, for it's an opportunity to learn,
And grow from experience, let it take its turn.
Verse 9:
Self-discipline is vital, to meet your goals,
Create a routine, and let it unfold,
Stay focused on your vision, and the prize,
For success is within reach, if you only try.
Verse 10:
In all that you do, let integrity guide,
Your actions and words, keep them aligned,
With honesty and transparency, pave your way,
For a trustworthy reputation, day by day.

CHAPTER TWELVE

The Path of Skill

Verse 1:
Freelancing demands skills diverse,
To succeed, one must always rehearse.
Build expertise in your chosen field,
For clients seek only the best yield.
Verse 2:
Develop your craft with utmost care,
Hone your skills, and never despair.
Keep learning, and never be done,
For knowledge is power, second to none.
Verse 3:
Practice your art with focus and zeal,
And make your work your most prized meal.
Perfect your skills with each passing day,
And soon, you'll be a master in every way.
Verse 4:
Embrace new technologies with delight,
And make them work for you with all your might.
Stay ahead of the curve, and be the trendsetter,
And soon, you'll be known as a real go-getter.
Verse 5:
Collaborate with others and learn new things,
From your peers, you'll find new wings.

Get feedback and improve your craft,
For learning is the key that makes you last.
Verse 6:
Remember, skills are the heart of freelancing,
Without them, success will remain entrancing.
So practice, learn, and perfect your trade,
And soon, clients will come in a parade.
Verse 7:
Strive for excellence in all that you do,
And success will come knocking for you.
Master your craft, and never give in,
And soon, you'll be the one who always wins.
Verse 8:
Skills are the foundation of every great career,
And freelancing is no exception, it's crystal clear.
So focus, learn, and always strive to improve,
And soon, you'll be the one who'll always groove.
Verse 9:
In the world of freelancing, skills are your sword,
Without them, you'll be lost, and your work will be ignored.
So sharpen your skills with every passing day,
And soon, success will come your way.
Verse 10:
Never stop learning, never stop growing,
For skills are the seeds of success worth sowing.
Strive for mastery in all that you do,
And soon, you'll be the one who'll always come through.

CHAPTER THIRTEEN

The Path of Discipline

Verse 1:

Do not let distractions sway,
Stay steadfast, focused every day,
With discipline, let your mind obey,
And success will come your way.
Verse 2:
Endlessly learn and grow,
Let your skills and knowledge show,
Always aim to improve and glow,
And opportunities will flow.
Verse 3:
Challenges come, but do not fret,
Embrace them, and do your best,
Through perseverance, you will get,
To heights beyond the rest.
Verse 4:
Build relationships with care and grace,
Network with those in your space,
Collaborate to win the race,
And establish your rightful place.
Verse 5:
Work hard, but also rest,
Take time for yourself, do what's best,

For a balanced life will attest,
To success, happiness, and zest.
Verse 6:
Act with integrity, be fair,
Honesty and ethics always there,
Professionalism beyond compare,
Will take you places everywhere.
Verse 7:
Opportunities come, take a chance,
With a calculated risk, advance,
Let your instincts lead the dance,
And success will enhance.
Verse 8:
Adapt to changes, embrace the new,
Opportunities will come through,
Innovation will always ensue,
And growth will follow in its queue.
Verse 9:
Time management is the key,
Set priorities with clarity,
Organize and work with efficiency,
And success will be your destiny.
Verse 10:
Celebrate success and milestones too,
Let them inspire and motivate you,
Learn from failures and mistakes too,
And success will follow through.

CHAPTER FOURTEEN

The Path of Self-Improvement

Verse 1:

Know thyself and your strengths, limitations,
Set goals to improve and hone your skills,
Seek new knowledge and embrace change,
For self-improvement is a lifelong process.
Verse 2:
Reflect on your past experiences and learn,
From mistakes and successes alike,
Let go of fear and embrace uncertainty,
And step outside your comfort zone.
Verse 3:
Embrace creativity and innovation,
And seek out inspiration from within and without,
Embody curiosity and passion in all you do,
And find joy in the journey of self-improvement.
Verse 4:
Cultivate discipline and focus your mind,
To overcome distractions and procrastination,
And achieve mastery through deliberate practice,
For excellence is not an act but a habit.
Verse 5:

Recognize the value of feedback and critique,
And use it to grow and develop,
Surround yourself with mentors and peers,
Who challenge and inspire you to be your best self.
Verse 6:
Embrace humility and a growth mindset,
And view failures as opportunities to learn,
Develop resilience and adaptability,
And become the best version of yourself.
Verse 7:
Let not the fear of failure consume you,
For every setback is a chance to renew.
Learn from your mistakes, let them guide,
And pave the path to success with pride.
Verse 8:
Embrace the power of collaboration,
And seek partnerships that bring innovation.
Together we can accomplish much more,
And reach greater heights than ever before.
Verse 9:
Never compromise on quality, for it is key,
To building a reputation that lasts eternally.
Strive for excellence in all that you do,
And the world will recognize and applaud you.
Verse 10:
Keep a positive attitude, come what may,
And face each challenge with courage every day.
Believe in yourself and your abilities,
And success will follow with ease and tranquility.
Verse 11:
Remember that freelancing is a journey,
Full of twists and turns that require tenacity.
Enjoy the ride, and savor every moment,

For the experience alone is a priceless component.

CHAPTER FIFTEEN

The Path of Perseverance

Verse 1:

With patience as your ally,
keep moving forward steadily.
Remember that great work takes time,
and success is often born of difficulty.
Verse 2:
Though obstacles may arise,
let them not impede your path.
Stay true to your vision and your skills,
and overcome challenges with unwavering resolve.
Verse 3:
For the road to success is rarely smooth,
and setbacks may come and go.
But with a steadfast heart and a clear mind,
you can push past adversity and continue to grow.
Verse 4:
Remember, too, the power of small steps,
and the value of consistent effort.
Every action you take, every task you complete,
brings you closer to your ultimate objective.
Verse 5:

Do not be discouraged by failures or setbacks,
for they are merely steps along the way.
With each stumble, you gain knowledge and experience,
that will ultimately aid you in your journey.
Verse 6:
Embrace challenges and the unknown,
for they offer opportunities to learn and improve.
Forge ahead with confidence, and the willingness to adapt,
and you will find yourself well-prepared for any future test.
Verse 7:
Let your work be fueled by passion and purpose,
and let your enthusiasm guide your steps.
When you love what you do, and why you do it,
success and fulfillment will surely follow.
Verse 8:
Be mindful, too, of balance and rest,
for these are essential to your well-being.
Take time to recharge, reflect, and renew,
and you will find yourself more productive and inspired.
Verse 9:
Above all, remember that perseverance is key,
and that success is often the fruit of patience and hard work.
With dedication, focus, and a clear sense of purpose,
you can achieve great things, and inspire others to do the same.
Verse 10:
So go forth with determination and purpose,
knowing that the path may be long and challenging.
But with each step, you come closer to your goal,
and with each success, you build a legacy of excellence.

CHAPTER SIXTEEN

Navigating the Challenges of Freelancing

Verse 1:

Be open to learning new skills,
It may take time, but it's worth the thrills,
Explore and experiment, don't be shy,
Continuous learning helps you soar high.
Verse 2:
Embrace the power of networking,
It's not just about connecting,
It's about building relationships strong,
That will help you all life long.
Verse 3:
Maintain a work-life balance,
It's key to prevent burnout and enhance,
Both your work and personal life,
That can help you thrive.
Verse 4:
Be proactive, take charge,
Don't let opportunities just barge,

Plan and prepare in advance,
That's how you seize the chance.
Verse 5:
Keep a track of your finances,
It's not just about taking chances,
A healthy financial state,
Is the key to a stress-free fate.
Verse 6:
Don't be afraid of competition,
It's the spice of the business mission,
Stay focused on your niche,
That's the way to reach your peak.
Verse 7:
Keep your communication clear,
It helps avoid any fear,
Both in your personal and professional sphere,
That's how you build trust sincere.
Verse 8:
Take care of your health and wellbeing,
It's not just about your wealth-building,
A healthy mind and body,
Is the way to a life of bounty.
Verse 9:
Stay humble and grounded,
It's the way to stay well-rounded,
Success is not just about money,
It's about a life that's full and sunny.
Verse 10:
Believe in yourself, have faith,
It's the way to conquer any wraith,
You have the power to create,
A life that's fulfilling and great.

CHAPTER SEVENTEEN

Nurturing Client Relationships for Freelancers

Verse 1:

As a freelancer, it's important to always strive for growth,

To continuously improve, learn and adapt as you go forth.

Set new challenges and goals to stay on track,

And don't be afraid to step out of your comfort zone and attack.

Verse 2:

Networking is key in the world of freelancing,

It opens up opportunities and enhances your understanding.

Connect with others in your field and beyond,

Building relationships that will help you respond.

Verse 3:

Communication is key when working on projects with clients,

Listen carefully to their needs and stay compliant.

Be responsive, clear and concise in your message,
And always strive to deliver work of the highest leverage.
Verse 4:
Time management is crucial for freelancers on the go,
Prioritize tasks and projects so you're always in the know.
Set boundaries and schedules to help you stay focused,
And don't forget to take breaks to help you stay composed.
Verse 5:
Managing finances is another key task,
Stay on top of invoices and taxes to avoid any backlash.
Invest in the right tools to help you manage your cash,
And always plan ahead to help you avoid any crash.
Verse 6:
Marketing is essential to grow your brand,
Craft a compelling message that will help you expand.
Create a portfolio that showcases your skills,
And don't forget to share it with clients for increased frills.
Verse 7:
Continuous learning is a must in this field,
Keep up with trends and new tools to yield.
Attend conferences and take online courses,
To help you improve and stay on top of resources.
Verse 8:
Remember to always stay true to your values and mission,
Building a brand that's authentic and driven.
Stay accountable and deliver on your promises,
And watch your reputation rise and flourish.
Verse 9:

Finally, never forget the power of persistence,
Success often comes to those who are consistent.
Stay focused, stay motivated, and keep moving forward,
And you'll find that your efforts will always be rewarded.

Verse 10:

Freelancing can be tough, but also incredibly rewarding,
With freedom and flexibility that's truly applauding.
Embrace the challenges and learn from the failures,
And always remember that success is truly contagious.

CHAPTER EIGHTEEN

The Importance of Networking

Verse 1:
Networking is crucial for a freelancer's success,
It helps to expand your reach and access,
Building relationships with clients and peers,
Is a valuable asset that will last for years.
Verse 2:
Attending events and joining groups,
Can help you build your brand and make some new loops,
Being active on social media platforms,
Can also help you to perform.
Verse 3:
Through networking, you may find,
Opportunities you never thought you'd find,
Potential clients and collaborators,
Can come from places you never expected to gather.
Verse 4:
Stay open and approachable,
To new contacts and opportunities that are probable,
It's not just about what you can gain,
But what you can give and help to maintain.

Verse 5:
Building relationships take time and effort,
It's important to be sincere and not just to slither,
Invest in building long-term connections,
And be open to learning from others' suggestions.
Verse 6:
Networking is a two-way street,
It requires give and take, a mutual treat,
Collaborate and share your expertise,
And be willing to learn from others with ease.
Verse 7:
Networking can help you stay relevant,
It provides a sense of community and contentment,
It can also help you stay updated,
On the latest trends and techniques that are highly rated.
Verse 8:
Networking can help you grow,
Both as an individual and as a pro,
It provides opportunities for personal development,
And a chance to showcase your talent.
Verse 9:
Networking can help you with support,
Through the ups and downs, a team effort to transport,
Building a community can help you find,
Mentors and friends, who have your best interest in mind.
Verse 10:
So, get out there and start connecting,
With people who are inspiring and engaging,
Networking is a powerful tool,
That can help you achieve your goals, as a whole.

CHAPTER NINETEEN

The Path to Success

Verse 1:

Success comes to those who seek it with dedication and hard work,

Who never lose sight of their goals and never let failure make them shirk,

Who are willing to learn and grow, and always strive to improve,

And never forget that success is a journey, not just a final move.

Verse 2:

Success is not just about making money or gaining fame,

It's about finding fulfillment in the work you do, and playing the game,

It's about making a positive impact on the world and leaving your mark,

And about being true to yourself and never letting your values go dark.

Verse 3:

To achieve success, you must have a clear vision of what you want,

And must be willing to take risks and face the challenges that may haunt,

You must be disciplined and focused, and always work with a plan,

And be willing to adapt and change, as the situation demands.

Verse 4:

Success is not a destination, but a journey that never ends,

And it requires constant effort and perseverance from your end,

It's about staying motivated and committed, even when things go rough,

And never losing sight of the bigger picture, no matter how tough.

Verse 5:

To succeed, you must surround yourself with people who inspire,

And who share your vision and values, and set your heart on fire,

You must seek out mentors and role models who can guide you along the way,

And always be open to learning and growing, no matter what they say.

Verse 6:

Success is not a solo journey, but a team effort that requires collaboration,

And a willingness to support and help others, without any hesitation,

It's about building relationships and networks, that can help you reach new heights,

And about giving back to the community, and making the world a better place in sight.

Verse 7:

To succeed, you must cultivate a mindset of abundance and positivity,

And let go of fear and self-doubt, that can hold you back from your destiny,

You must focus on your strengths and talents, and use them to create value,

And be willing to innovate and experiment, and explore the unknown avenue.

Verse 8:

Success is not a one-time achievement, but a continuous process of evolution,

And it requires a constant willingness to learn and seek new solutions,

It's about staying humble and grounded, even when you have reached great heights,

And about being grateful and mindful, of the blessings that come in your sights.

Verse 9:

To succeed, you must never give up or lose hope, no matter how bleak it may seem,

And always keep your eyes on the prize, even when things don't go as per your dream,

You must trust in yourself and your abilities, and believe in your potential and power,

And never let anyone else's opinion or judgement make you feel sour.

Verse 10:

Success is not a final destination, but a continuous journey of growth and transformation,

And it requires a constant willingness to embrace change and adaptation,

It's about staying true to yourself and your values, and living a life of purpose and meaning,

And about making a difference in the world, and leaving behind a legacy worth seeing.

CHAPTER TWENTY

List of Freelance websites

1. Upwork - https://www.upwork.com/
2. Freelancer - https://www.freelancer.com/
3. Fiverr - https://www.fiverr.com/
4. Guru - https://www.guru.com/
5. Toptal - https://www.toptal.com/
6. 99designs - https://99designs.com/
7. PeoplePerHour - https://www.peopleperhour.com/
8. SimplyHired - https://www.simplyhired.com/
9. FlexJobs - https://www.flexjobs.com/
10. DesignCrowd - https://www.designcrowd.com/
11. Freelance Writing - https://www.freelancewriting.com/
12. Writer Access - https://www.writeraccess.com/
13. Textbroker - https://www.textbroker.com/
14. Scripted - https://www.scripted.com/
15. Skyword - https://www.skyword.com/
16. Hirable - https://www.hirable.com/
17. Nexxt - https://www.nexxt.com/
18. SolidGigs - https://solidgigs.com/
19. Project4hire - https://www.project4hire.com/

20. SimplyBook - https://simplybook.me/en/
21. Crowdsource - https://www.crowdsource.com/
22. Truelancer - https://www.truelancer.com/
23. Workhoppers - https://www.workhoppers.com/
24. ProBlogger - https://problogger.com/
25. Working Nomads - https://www.workingnomads.co/jobs
26. Outsourcely - https://www.outsourcely.com/
27. iWriter - https://www.iwriter.com/
28. Hirable - https://www.hirable.com/
29. Gun.io - https://gun.io/
30. Zeerk - https://zeerk.com/
31. SEO Clerks - https://www.seoclerk.com/
32. Writer Access - https://www.writeraccess.com/
33. Writer Bay - https://writerbay.com/
34. FreelancerMap - https://www.freelancermap.com/
35. Beesy.pro - https://beesy.pro/
36. Rent a Coder - https://www.rent-acoder.com/
37. iFreelance - https://www.ifreelance.com/
38. All Freelance Writing - https://allfreelancewriting.com/
39. Aquent - https://aquent.com/
40. Hireable - https://www.hireable.com/
41. GetACoder - https://www.getacoder.com/
42. Crowded - https://www.crowded.com/
43. Hirable - https://www.hirable.com/
44. Gigster - https://gigster.com/
45. Freelance Writing Jobs - https://www.freelancewritingjobs.ca/
46. Workana - https://www.workana.com/
47. FreeUp - https://freeup.net/
48. Artisan Talent - https://artisantalent.com/
49. TopCoder - https://www.topcoder.com/

50. OnSite - https://onsite.io/
51. GigBucks - https://gigbucks.com/
52. CloudPeeps - https://www.cloudpeeps.com/
53. DesignHill - https://www.designhill.com/
54. LocalSolo - https://localsolo.com/
55. Sologig - https://www.sologig.com/
56. Hire My Mom - https://www.hiremymom.com/
57. Remotive - https://remotive.io/

Marketing Neeti for

Chief Marketing Officers

CHAPTER TWENTY-ONE

The Confrontation of Marketing Challenges

Verse 1:

Amidst the sea of marketing challenges,
Stand thou, the CMO, with courage and will,
Tireless in thy efforts, unwavering in thy vision,
Leading thy team to fulfill the company's mission.
Verse 2:
As the market trends ebb and flow like the tides,
Stay vigilant, agile, and adapt with ease,
For in times of change, lies the greatest of opportunities,
To seize and carve a niche that none can seize.
Verse 3:
The customer is the heart of thy endeavor,
Study their needs and desires with a sharp gaze,
Design products and services that cater to their wants,
Build trust and loyalty that none can raze.
Verse 4:
Collaboration is the key to success,
Engage with thy colleagues, thy team, and thy peers,
Harness their talents, their knowledge, their zeal,
Forge partnerships that last beyond the years.
Verse 5:

Measure thy progress with a keen eye,
Metrics and data, thy allies in the quest,
Analyze and learn from successes and failures,
Refine thy strategies, and put them to the test.

Verse 6:

The competition may seem daunting,
But fear not, for thy spirit is strong,
With creativity, innovation, and passion,
Thou shalt emerge victorious, where others have gone wrong.

Verse 7:

Stay true to thy values and principles,
Ethics, integrity, and honesty, thy guiding light,
For in the end, it's not just about profit and gain,
But also about making a positive impact that shines bright.

Verse 8:

Remember, O CMO, that the journey is long,
With many a challenge, setback, and strife,
But with faith in thyself and the team by thy side,
Thou shalt overcome, and lead a successful life.

Verse 9:

Those who are wise in the ways of marketing,
See the market as a vast ocean, with currents ever-changing.
To succeed, one must navigate the tides with skill and strategy,
And stay attuned to the shifting needs and desires of the consumer.

Verse 10:

As a CMO, you are the captain of your ship,
Leading your crew through stormy seas and uncharted waters.

With a clear vision and a steady hand,

You can guide your business to success, and leave a lasting impact on the world.

CHAPTER TWENTY-TWO

The Path to Effective Marketing

Verse 1:
With every step we take,
Our journey in marketing, we make,
Success lies in planning ahead,
Without which, we'll be left in dread.
Verse 2:
Marketing is more than just a skill,
It requires passion, hard work and will,
Knowing your customers is a must,
Only then, can you gain their trust.
Verse 3:
Set goals that are clear and defined,
With tactics that are well-refined,
Be flexible in your approach,
And adapt to the market, encroach.
Verse 4:
Branding is not just about design,
It's the story you tell that will shine,
Connect with your audience, be true,
And they will resonate with you.
Verse 5:

Innovation and creativity,
Are key to staying ahead, undoubtedly,
Embrace change and new technology,
And lead your team with vision and strategy.
Verse 6:
Collaborate with your team,
And together, you'll achieve your dream,
Communication is key to success,
And teamwork will always impress.
Verse 7:
Keep a watchful eye on your competition,
But never lose sight of your own mission,
Stay true to your values and vision,
And success will come with precision.
Verse 8:
Measure and analyze your performance,
And make improvements with confidence,
Continuously learn and adapt,
And success will follow, that's a fact.
Verse 9:
In marketing, mistakes will be made,
But it's how you handle them that will pave,
The path to success and growth,
And earn you the respect of both.
Verse 10:
In this journey of marketing, remember,
To be humble, open-minded, and tender,
To learn from your mistakes and grow,
And let your passion and hard work show.

CHAPTER TWENTY-THREE

The Importance of Market Research

Verse 1:

Without market research, a CMO's vision is blind,
A foundation of knowledge is what they must find.
Know the target audience and their needs,
This will help develop marketing strategies that succeed.
Verse 2:
Market research will reveal the competition,
Their strengths, their weaknesses, and their position.
Understand the market trends and where they lead,
This will help CMOs to plan and take the lead.
Verse 3:
Market research also includes social media,
Know how to use it to reach a wider idea.
What platforms are popular, where is the buzz,
These insights will make the CMOs job less of a fuss.
Verse 4:
Market research is ongoing, it's never done,
Keep a close eye, watch and listen to everyone.
Stay on top of trends, adapt to change,
This is how a CMO's success will range.
Verse 5:

Invest in market research, it's worth the cost,

It will save you from making marketing mistakes and getting lost.

Allocate time, money, and resources with care,

And the business will thrive, with a strong brand to share.

Verse 6:

Market research is not just about numbers and stats,

It's also about understanding emotions and where they're at.

Know the pain points and the desires of your target,

This will help create campaigns that truly connect.

Verse 7:

Keep an open mind, and don't be afraid to pivot,

The market may change, and you must be quick to fit it.

Don't be stuck in old ways, or afraid to take a risk,

Adapt, innovate, and the brand will truly brisk.

Verse 8:

Remember, market research is not a one-time deal,

It's an ongoing process, that will make you seal.

Stay curious, stay updated, and stay informed,

This is how a CMO's success will be adorned.

Verse 9:

Market research is the foundation of any good plan,

It will guide the business, and help it expand.

Be thorough, be diligent, and be strategic,

And the brand's success will be long-term and terrific.

Verse 10:

The power of market research cannot be denied,

It will help the business grow, and its reach multiply.

Embrace it, use it, and make it your ally,

And the CMO's success will soar, like a sky so high.

CHAPTER TWENTY-FOUR

Building a Strong Brand Identity

Verse 1:

A strong brand identity is key,
It sets you apart and makes customers see.
A clear message that speaks to your target,
This is how your brand can truly impact.
Verse 2:
Your brand is more than just a logo or name,
It's the essence of your business, its claim to fame.
It's what people think and feel about your company,
So make sure your brand represents you accurately.
Verse 3:
To build a strong brand, you must define your values,
What your business stands for, what it values.
A clear brand purpose and mission,
This will give your brand a strong position.
Verse 4:
Your brand identity must be consistent,
From the logo to the messaging, it's persistent.
Your brand should be easily recognized,
And evoke positive emotions, it's a prize.
Verse 5:

Consistency is key, but so is creativity,
Your brand should be unique and show individuality.
Don't be afraid to take risks and try something new,
This is how your brand can break through.

Verse 6:

Your brand identity should be reflected in everything you do,
From your website to your social media too.
Make sure your brand is present and clear,
This is how you can make your competition fear.

Verse 7:

Your employees should embody your brand identity,
They should live and breathe it with sincerity.
This will ensure that your brand is consistent and true,
And customers will trust and stick with you.

Verse 8:

Building a strong brand identity takes time,
But it's worth it to create a brand that truly shines.
Invest in your brand and keep it strong,
And your business will prosper all along.

Verse 9:

Remember, your brand is your identity,
It's what makes your business stand out and be,
So take the time to define and refine it,
And your brand will become a true hit.

Verse 10:

Building a strong brand identity is a journey,
But with persistence and dedication, you'll earn the attorney.
Your brand will be the one that customers choose,
And your business will win and never lose.

CHAPTER TWENTY-FIVE

The Power of Branding

Verse 1:
Branding is the identity of a business,
It's how customers perceive and bear witness.
It's the essence of the company's personality,
And the message it sends to its community.
Verse 2:
A strong brand builds trust and loyalty,
It's the key to building a lasting legacy.
It sets a business apart from the rest,
And gives it a competitive edge that's best.
Verse 3:
A brand is more than just a logo,
It's the values and beliefs that make it glow.
It's the emotional connection it creates,
And the experience it provides that resonates.
Verse 4:
Branding is an ongoing process,
It's not something that happens with one progress.
It evolves and grows as the business does,
And adapts to changing markets with ease and buzz.
Verse 5:
To build a brand, consistency is key,
From the message to the imagery that we see.

Make sure the brand is reflected in everything,
And customers will remember and make it their thing.
Verse 6:
A strong brand can withstand tough times,
And will continue to thrive and make chimes.
It's an investment worth the effort,
And the rewards will be abundant and assert.
Verse 7:
Branding is a way to connect with people,
To communicate and create a bond that's simple.
It's the heart and soul of a business's identity,
And the cornerstone of its long-term prosperity.
Verse 8:
A brand should be unique and memorable,
With a story that's engaging and so admirable.
It should evoke emotions and create an experience,
That customers will cherish and share with insistence.
Verse 9:
A powerful brand can inspire action,
And create a sense of satisfaction.
It can make customers feel like they belong,
And keep them coming back all lifelong.
Verse 10:
In conclusion, branding is a vital part,
Of a business's success and its heart.
It's a never-ending journey that we embark,
And with the right strategy, we'll make our mark.

CHAPTER TWENTY-SIX

Nurturing a Creative Team

Verse 1:

A CMO must create a team of creativity,
Encourage ideas, let them flow with agility.
Diverse skills and backgrounds, they should bring,
With collaboration and trust, they will make anything.
Verse 2:
Creativity needs space to breathe and thrive,
Let the team take risks, let them come alive.
A safe environment that welcomes the new,
This is where the team will shine through.
Verse 3:
Provide the tools, the resources they need,
Invest in training, and they will exceed.
Encourage experimentation, welcome mistakes,
This will make the team stronger and their growth rate.
Verse 4:
Celebrate successes, learn from failures,
The team will learn, adapt, and become trailblazers.
Nurture their talents, and they will soar,
And make the CMO's vision more and more.
Verse 5:

A creative team must also be happy,
Keep them motivated, let them feel snappy.
Incentives, recognition, and fun activities,
These will make the team's life less dull and dreary.
Verse 6:
Remember, a creative team is a valuable asset,
They make the CMO's vision a reality, and that's a fact.
Nurture their talent, their passion, and their drive,
And watch them make your business thrive.
Verse 7:
Marketing metrics are the key to success,
Tracking and analyzing to make progress.
Measure ROI, conversion rates, and more,
This data will guide your marketing score.
Verse 8:
The right marketing mix is the ultimate goal,
A balance of tactics to achieve the whole.
From SEO to social media and events,
Each has a role that can enhance your presence.
Verse 9:
Collaboration is crucial to marketing's growth,
Work with cross-functional teams and it will show.
Sales, product, and design - they all play a part,
Together they can make an impact that's smart.
Verse 10:
Continuous improvement is the final step,
Always striving to be better with each rep.
Learning from successes and failures alike,
A CMO's journey is never done, but it's worth the hike.

CHAPTER TWENTY-SEVEN

Creating a Strategic Marketing Campaign

Verse 1:

Define the goals and objectives of the campaign,
What do you want to achieve, what's the aim?
Know the target audience, their needs and desires,
This is how to develop marketing that inspires.
Verse 2:
Conduct market research to understand the market,
Analyze trends, competition, and what's happening in it.
Develop a unique value proposition,
This is how to differentiate from the competition.
Verse 3:
Choose the right channels to reach the audience,
Social media, email, or traditional methods can enhance.
Create a message that resonates with the audience,
This is how to generate engagement and influence.
Verse 4:
Develop a budget and allocate resources,
Monitor and measure progress to stay on course.
Be agile and adjust as necessary,
This is how to lead a successful campaign with clarity.
Verse 5:

Collaborate with internal and external teams,
Maximize resources and share knowledge it seems.
Create a timeline and assign responsibilities,
This is how to create a plan with effective capabilities.
Verse 6:
Set benchmarks to measure performance,
Identify KPIs to track and enhance.
Be aware of limitations and potential risks,
This is how to create a plan with strategic twists.
Verse 7:
Identify the key performance indicators,
Metrics to track progress and success factors.
Know when to pivot, when to persevere,
This is how to avoid marketing campaign disasters.
Verse 8:
Collaborate with cross-functional teams,
Marketing is not done in isolation, it seems.
Involve stakeholders to ensure buy-in,
This is how to ensure the campaign will win.
Verse 9:
Test and iterate, don't be afraid to fail,
Learning from mistakes is how to prevail.
Embrace innovation, take risks to stand out,
This is how to create a campaign with clout.
Verse 10:
Lastly, measure and analyze the results,
Did you achieve the goals, did it have the desired jolt?
Gather insights and lessons learned,
This is how to continuously improve and discern.

CHAPTER TWENTY-EIGHT

Measuring Marketing Success

Verse 1:

Marketing success is not just a feeling,
It must be measured for better understanding.
Key performance indicators are the way to go,
Tracking progress and seeing the results flow.

Verse 2:

Identify metrics that align with your goals,
This will help to measure and assess your roles.
Examples include website traffic, engagement, and conversion,
These metrics can provide insight and be the key to decision.

Verse 3:

Be specific in your measurement approach,
Consistency is key, don't just take a quick approach.
Track over time, month to month and year over year,
This is how to see progress and adjust marketing gear.

Verse 4:

Analyze data and interpret the results,
Understand what's working and what needs to be consult.

This is the basis for marketing optimization,
Use data-driven insights for strategic implementation.
Verse 5:
Share results with the marketing team,
Transparency is important, let them see the scheme.
This will keep everyone aligned and focused,
Towards the goals that the campaign has posted.
Verse 6:
Adjust and refine the marketing plan,
Make changes that are based on the data on hand.
Keep testing and optimizing for better results,
This is how to achieve marketing success that tumults.
Verse 7:
Celebrate the successes along the way,
Acknowledge and recognize the efforts of the day.
But don't rest on your laurels, keep pushing ahead,
This is how to maintain a successful marketing tread.
Verse 8:
In conclusion, measuring marketing success is key,
To understanding the impact of your strategy.
With data-driven insights, you can optimize and improve,
And lead your organization to achieve marketing moves.
Verse 9:
Don't be afraid to take risks and try something new,
Innovation and creativity can lead to breakthroughs.
Learn from failures, embrace the lessons they teach,
This is how to evolve and stay within your reach.
Verse 10:
Marketing is about people, and how they feel,
Connection, empathy, and authenticity are real.
Be genuine, transparent, and build trust,

This is how to succeed and create marketing that's a must

CHAPTER TWENTY-NINE

Digital Marketing Automation Websites

1. HubSpot - https://www.hubspot.com/
2. Marketo - https://www.marketo.com/
3. Pardot - https://www.pardot.com/
4. ActiveCampaign - https://www.activecampaign.com/
5. Eloqua - https://www.oracle.com/marketingcloud/products/marketing-automation/eloqua/
6. Infusionsoft - https://www.keap.com/infusionsoft
7. Drip - https://www.drip.com/
8. Ontraport - https://ontraport.com/
9. Act-On - https://www.act-on.com/
10. Autopilot - https://www.autopilothq.com/
11. SharpSpring - https://sharpspring.com/
12. Mailchimp - https://mailchimp.com/
13. AWeber - https://www.aweber.com/
14. GetResponse - https://www.getresponse.com/
15. Constant Contact - https://www.constantcontact.com/
16. Campaign Monitor - https://www.campaignmonitor.com/
17. Sendinblue - https://www.sendinblue.com/
18. Klaviyo - https://www.klaviyo.com/

19. ConvertKit - https://convertkit.com/
20. Keap - https://keap.com/
21. SendX - https://www.sendx.io/
22. Salesfusion - https://www.salesfusion.com/
23. MarketSharp - https://www.marketsharp.com/
24. SalesNexus - https://www.salesnexus.com/
25. Net-Results - https://www.net-results.com/
26. LeadSquared - https://www.leadsquared.com/
27. Ontrapages - https://ontrapages.com/
28. SalesManago - https://www.salesmanago.com/
29. SALESmanago - https://app.salesmanago.com/
30. Omnisend - https://www.omnisend.com/
31. Wishpond - https://www.wishpond.com/
32. iContact - https://www.icontact.com/
33. Emarsys - https://emarsys.com/
34. CleverTap - https://clevertap.com/
35. Drift - https://www.drift.com/
36. WebEngage - https://webengage.com/
37. Intercom - https://www.intercom.com/
38. Freshmarketer - https://www.freshworks.com/marketing-automation/
39. Salesforce Marketing Cloud - https://www.salesforce.com/products/marketing-cloud/overview/
40. IBM Watson Campaign Automation - https://www.ibm.com/products/watson-campaign-automation
41. Maropost - https://www.maropost.com/
42. Iterable - https://iterable.com/
43. Customer.io - https://customer.io/
44. Moosend - https://moosend.com/
45. SendPulse - https://sendpulse.com/
46. Zoho Campaigns - https://www.zoho.com/campaigns/

47. EngageBay - https://www.engagebay.com/
48. Pabbly Email Marketing - https://www.pabbly.com/email-marketing/
49. Leadsius - https://www.leadsius.com/
50. Campaigner - https://www.campaigner.com/
51. Experiture - https://experiture.com/
52. CleverReach - https://www.cleverreach.com/
53. Benchmark Email - https://www.benchmarkemail.com/
54. Salesflare - https://salesflare.com/
55. SendGrid - https://sendgrid.com/
56. Elastic Email - https://elasticemail.com/
57. Zapier - https://zapier.com/

CHAPTER THIRTY

Other Marketing Websites

1. Jumplead - https://jumplead.com/
2. Pardot - https://www.pardot.com/
3. Maropost - https://www.maropost.com/
4. Selligent - https://www.selligent.com/
5. LeadSquared - https://www.leadsquared.com/
6. Drift - https://www.drift.com/
7. Net-Results - https://www.net-results.com/
8. Marketo - https://www.marketo.com/
9. Autopilot - https://www.autopilothq.com/
10. Instapage - https://instapage.com/
11. Intercom - https://www.intercom.com/
12. Leadfeeder - https://www.leadfeeder.com/
13. Act-On - https://www.act-on.com/
14. Drip - https://www.drip.com/
15. Salesfusion - https://www.salesfusion.com/
16. SharpSpring - https://sharpspring.com/
17. HubSpot - https://www.hubspot.com/
18. Zoho MarketingHub - https://www.zoho.com/marketinghub/
19. GetResponse - https://www.getresponse.com/

20. Iterable - https://iterable.com/
21. Infusionsoft - https://www.infusionsoft.com/
22. SalesLoft - https://salesloft.com/
23. Sendinblue - https://www.sendinblue.com/
24. Ontraport - https://ontraport.com/
25. ActiveCampaign - https://www.activecampaign.com/
26. Sharpspring - https://sharpspring.com/
27. AWeber - https://www.aweber.com/
28. Eloqua - https://www.oracle.com/marketingcloud/products/marketing-automation/eloqua/
29. Omnisend - https://www.omnisend.com/
30. Salesflare - https://salesflare.com/
31. WebEngage - https://webengage.com/
32. Salesforce Marketing Cloud - https://www.salesforce.com/products/marketing-cloud/overview/
33. Infusionsoft by Keap - https://keap.com/product/infusionsoft
34. MarketMuse - https://marketmuse.com/
35. ConvertKit - https://convertkit.com/
36. Lead Liaison - https://www.leadliaison.com/
37. SendX - https://www.sendx.io/
38. Zaius - https://www.zaius.com/
39. Customer.io - https://customer.io/
40. Wishpond - https://www.wishpond.com/
41. Databox - https://databox.com/
42. Moosend - https://moosend.com/
43. Driftrock - https://www.driftrock.com/
44. Salesmate - https://www.salesmate.io/
45. Klaviyo - https://www.klaviyo.com/
46. SalesNexus - https://salesnexus.com/
47. Actito - https://www.actito.com/en
48. Agile CRM - https://www.agilecrm.com/

49. Salesfusion - https://www.salesfusion.com/
50. ClickDimensions - https://clickdimensions.com/
51. BrandMaker - https://www.brandmaker.com/
52. Experiture - https://experiture.com/
53. OutboundEngine - https://www.outboundengine.com/
54. SimplyCast - https://www.simplycast.com/
55. dotdigital Engagement Cloud - https://dotdigital.com/
56. Mailchimp - https://mailchimp.com/
57. Campaign Monitor - https://www.campaignmonitor.com/

CHAPTER THIRTY-ONE

AI Lead Generation Websites

1. LeadSquared - https://www.leadsquared.com/
2. SalesOptimize - https://www.salesoptimize.com/
3. Conversica - https://www.conversica.com/
4. Xant - https://www.xant.ai/
5. Zoho CRM - https://www.zoho.com/crm/
6. Clearbit - https://clearbit.com/
7. Visitor Queue - https://visitorqueue.com/
8. Hubspot - https://www.hubspot.com/
9. Albacross - https://albacross.com/
10. Drift - https://www.drift.com/
11. LeadCrunch - https://www.leadcrunch.com/
12. Netline Corporation - https://www.netline.com/
13. SalesIntel - https://salesintel.io/
14. Prospecting.io - https://prospecting.io/
15. Unomy - https://unomy.com/
16. Ocean.io - https://ocean.io/
17. Leadberry - https://www.leadberry.com/
18. InsideView - https://www.insideview.com/
19. Alore - https://alore.io/

20. LinkedIn Sales Navigator - https://www.linkedin.com/sales
21. D&B Hoovers - https://www.dnb.com/products/marketing-sales.html
22. Apollo.io - https://www.apollo.io/
23. UpLead - https://www.uplead.com/
24. Outreach.io - https://www.outreach.io/
25. SalesLeads.ai - https://www.salesleads.ai/
26. ZoomInfo - https://www.zoominfo.com/
27. 6sense - https://6sense.com/
28. EverString - https://www.everstring.com/
29. People.ai - https://people.ai/
30. LeadGnome - https://leadgnome.com/
31. Drip - https://www.drip.com/
32. MadKudu - https://www.madkudu.com/
33. LimeLeads - https://www.limeleads.com/
34. PersistIQ - https://persistiq.com/
35. DiscoverOrg - https://discoverorg.com/
36. AeroLeads - https://aeroleads.com/
37. FullContact - https://www.fullcontact.com/
38. Lusha - https://www.lusha.com/
39. LeadIQ - https://leadiq.com/
40. Infer - https://infer.com/
41. KiteDesk - https://www.kitedesk.com/
42. Leadfeeder - https://www.leadfeeder.com/
43. Salesfusion - https://www.salesfusion.com/
44. Marketo - https://www.marketo.com/
45. Pardot - https://www.pardot.com/
46. Act-On - https://www.act-on.com/
47. Eloqua - https://www.oracle.com/marketingcloud/products/marketing-automation/eloqua/
48. SharpSpring - https://sharpspring.com/
49. Sendinblue - https://www.sendinblue.com/

50. Autopilot - https://www.autopilothq.com/
51. Ontraport - https://ontraport.com/
52. Mautic - https://www.mautic.org/
53. Infusionsoft - https://keap.com/infusionsoft
54. GetResponse - https://www.getresponse.com/
55. Campaign Monitor - https://www.campaignmonitor.com/
56. Emma - https://myemma.com/
57. ActiveCampaign - https://www.activecampaign.com/
58. Salesflare - https://salesflare.com/
59. Agile CRM - https://www.agilecrm.com/

CHAPTER THIRTY-TWO

Social Media Marketing Websites

1. Hootsuite - https://hootsuite.com/
2. Buffer - https://buffer.com/
3. Sprout Social - https://sproutsocial.com/
4. MeetEdgar - https://meetedgar.com/
5. Later - https://later.com/
6. AgoraPulse - https://www.agorapulse.com/
7. Sendible - https://www.sendible.com/
8. SocialPilot - https://www.socialpilot.co/
9. Loomly - https://www.loomly.com/
10. CoSchedule - https://coschedule.com/
11. Planoly - https://www.planoly.com/
12. Iconosquare - https://www.iconosquare.com/
13. Tailwind - https://www.tailwindapp.com/
14. SocialFlow - https://www.socialflow.com/
15. Sked Social - https://skedsocial.com/
16. Planable - https://planable.io/
17. Crowdfire - https://www.crowdfireapp.com/
18. Falcon.io - https://www.falcon.io/
19. Khoros - https://khoros.com/
20. SocialOomph - https://www.socialoomph.com/

21. SocialBee - https://socialbee.io/
22. Kontentino - https://www.kontentino.com/
23. SocialChamp - https://www.socialchamp.io/
24. PromoRepublic - https://promorepublic.com/
25. SendSocialMedia - https://sendsocialmedia.com/
26. Agorapulse - https://www.agorapulse.com/
27. Edgar - https://meetedgar.com/
28. Social Pilot - https://www.socialpilot.co/
29. Sprinklr - https://www.sprinklr.com/
30. Social Report - https://www.socialreport.com/
31. NapoleonCat - https://napoleoncat.com/
32. Brand24 - https://brand24.com/
33. Quintly - https://www.quintly.com/
34. MavSocial - https://mavsocial.com/
35. Oktopost - https://www.oktopost.com/
36. Brandwatch - https://www.brandwatch.com/
37. BuzzSumo - https://buzzsumo.com/
38. Zoho Social - https://www.zoho.com/social/
39. MeetFrank - https://meetfrank.com/
40. BrandCrowd - https://www.brandcrowd.com/
41. Socialbakers - https://www.socialbakers.com/
42. Social Insider - https://www.socialinsider.io/
43. Planable - https://planable.io/
44. Kuku.io - https://kuku.io/
45. ViralTag - https://www.viraltag.com/
46. HeyOrca - https://heyorca.com/
47. TweetDeck - https://tweetdeck.twitter.com/
48. Canva - https://www.canva.com/
49. Followerwonk - https://followerwonk.com/
50. Oktopost - https://www.oktopost.com/
51. Later - https://later.com/
52. Sendible - https://www.sendible.com/
53. MissingLettr - https://missinglettr.com/

54. PromoRepublic - https://promorepublic.com/
55. SocialPilot - https://www.socialpilot.co/
56. Crowdfire - https://www.crowdfireapp.com/
57. Hopper HQ - https://www.hopperhq.com/
58. Agora Pulse - https://www.agorapulse.com/
59. Meet Edgar - https://meetedgar.com/
60. Zapier – https://zapier.com

CTO Neeti for

Chief Technology Officers

CHAPTER THIRTY-THREE

The Importance of Technology Leadership

Verse 1:

Technology is an ever-changing field,
CTOs must be flexible and ready to yield.
Embrace change, stay ahead of the game,
This is how to lead with innovation and fame.

Verse 2:

Understand the business, its goals and its vision,
Technology should support and enhance its mission.
CTOs must align the tech with the business,
This is how to bring value and success with finesse.

Verse 3:

Stay up to date with the latest trends,
New innovations and tech will soon be trends.
Research and experiment with new tools and platforms,
This is how to keep the business on top with strong norms.

Verse 4:

Collaborate with other teams across the organization,
Understand their needs and provide the right solutions.
CTOs must be strategic and think ahead,
This is how to lead with innovation and be widespread.

Verse 7:

A CTO must balance the needs of today,
While also planning for the future in every way.
Adapt to changes and embrace innovation,
This is the path to a successful technology implementation.

Verse 8:

Technology must be secure, reliable, and scalable,
To meet the demands of customers, stakeholders, and the table.
Stay up-to-date with industry trends and best practices,
This is how to build technology with long-term success.

Verse 9:

Collaboration is key, with teams both far and wide,
Bring everyone together and take their insights in stride.
Empower your team and let them take the lead,
This is how to build technology that everyone will need.

Verse 10:

A CTO's job is never done, there's always more to do,
Stay passionate, stay focused, and always follow through.
Lead with integrity, honor, and grace,
This is how to leave your mark on the technology race.

CHAPTER THIRTY-FOUR

Embracing Technology for Growth

Verse 1:

The role of a CTO is to drive technology,
Innovative solutions for business productivity.
Analyze the current tech infrastructure,
And recommend upgrades for greater allure.

Verse 2:

A CTO must think strategically,
How to use technology to reach new capacity.
This requires research and development,
To keep the business ahead of competitors.

Verse 3:

Technology trends are ever-changing,
A CTO must stay updated and keep innovating.
Know what's new and what's trending,
And integrate it into the business planning.

Verse 4:

Technology is not just about hardware and software,
It's also about automation, AI and data to share.
A CTO must develop a comprehensive plan,
To ensure that the business stays ahead of the game.

Verse 5:

Effective communication is key,
To ensure that the tech plan is implemented seamlessly.
Collaboration between teams is crucial,
Verse 6:
A CTO must be a visionary,
To see the possibilities and opportunities.
Not just for today, but for the future,
To ensure that the business stays on the adventure.
Verse 7:
Technology can be a catalyst for growth,
But only if it's implemented with care and both.
A CTO must lead with purpose and passion,
To ensure that the business stays on the fashion.
Verse 8:
Integrating technology into business processes,
Can lead to greater efficiency and progress.
A CTO must be mindful of the risks,
And ensure that the business is well-equipped.
Verse 9:
The role of a CTO is ever-evolving,
To meet the needs of a business problem-solving.
To stay on top, a CTO must be flexible and adaptive,
To ensure that the business stays competitive.
Verse 10:
In conclusion, a CTO is the driving force,
To ensure that a business stays on course.
By embracing technology and leading with vision,
The CTO can ensure that the business thrives with precision.

CHAPTER THIRTY-FIVE

The Importance of Teamwork

Verse 1:

As a CTO, it's not just about your skill,
Collaboration and teamwork are the key to fulfill.
Gather the right team, each with their own strength,
Together you can go to any length.
Verse 2:
Communication is the key to success,
Share your vision, goals, and progress.
Be transparent, honest, and clear,
This will build trust and eliminate fear.
Verse 3:
Listen to your team, hear what they say,
Value their input, don't just brush it away.
Each member brings a unique perspective,
This diversity will make your team effective.
Verse 4:
Delegate tasks, empower your team,
This will create a culture of self-esteem.
Encourage growth and provide support,
This will help your team to excel and report.
Verse 5:

Celebrate successes, learn from failures,
This will help your team to be future trailblazers.
Foster a culture of continuous learning,
This will keep your team innovating and yearning.
Verse 6:
Motivate your team, inspire them to aim high,
Provide them with opportunities to reach for the sky.
Together you can achieve great things,
This is the power of teamwork's wings.
Verse 7:
Collaborate with other teams, don't work in silos,
Communication is key to avoid any woes.
Understand the business, its values, and goals,
This will help align your technology role.
Verse 8:
Stay up-to-date with the latest trends,
Technology is constantly evolving, and innovation never ends.
Stay curious and keep learning,
This is how you'll keep your skills from turning.
Verse 9:
Stay organized and manage your time,
Prioritize tasks, so everything is in line.
Delegate and empower your team,
This is how to manage technology with a winning scheme.
Verse 10:
Measure and track progress to see the impact,
Technology can help drive the business's growth in fact.
Identify areas for improvement and optimization,
This is how to lead technology with precision.

CHAPTER THIRTY-SIX

Hiring and Retaining Top Talent

Verse 1:
Hiring tech talent is a top priority,
Find the right people to build your team with authority.
Look for skills, experience, and cultural fit,
This is how to make sure they will be a good fit.
Verse 2:
Start with a clear job description,
Communicate the responsibilities and mission.
Use assessments and tests to evaluate their skills,
This is how to make sure they have the right thrills.
Verse 3:
Be transparent about the company's vision,
Make sure they understand the mission.
Provide opportunities for growth and development,
This is how to retain and keep talent with sentiment.
Verse 4:
Create a positive and inclusive work culture,
Make sure it's diverse and full of nurture.
Celebrate achievements and recognize success,
This is how to create a high-performing tech team with finesse.

Verse 5:

When facing challenges, stay calm and composed,
For panic and frustration will leave you exposed.
Keep your mind open and receptive to change,
And you'll find solutions within your range.

Verse 6:

Collaborate with your team to build a strong foundation,
Trust and respect are the keys to great communication.
Empower your team and provide them with the right tools,
And watch as they accomplish great feats and break through walls.

Verse 7:

Stay updated with the latest trends and innovations,
Technology is ever-changing and brings new implications.
Embrace new ideas and be willing to experiment,
This is how to keep your company relevant.

Verse 8:

Strive for excellence in all that you do,
And success will follow you through and through.
But never forget your moral compass and values,
For they guide you through tough choices and conflicts.

Verse 9:

Remember, you are not just a CTO but a leader,
And your actions and decisions impact the entire enterprise.
Lead with integrity, purpose, and passion,
And watch as your team achieves greatness and thrives.

CHAPTER THIRTY-SEVEN

Fostering a Collaborative Culture

Verse 1:

Encourage open communication and feedback,
It helps to build trust and make progress.
Create an inclusive environment where all voices are heard,
This is how to build a team that's united and not deterred.

Verse 2:

Collaborate on problem-solving and decision-making,
Involve team members to avoid any mistaking.
Celebrate achievements and acknowledge effort,
This is how to build a culture that's positive and not snort.

Verse 3:

Encourage learning and development opportunities,
Help team members to enhance their capabilities.
Provide mentorship and coaching to foster growth,
This is how to build a team that's constantly on the go.

Verse 4:

Embrace diversity and inclusion as a core value,
It brings a wealth of ideas that's not so few.

Create a safe space for all team members to share,

This is how to build a culture that's inclusive and not rare.

Verse 6:

Strive to improve your communication skills,

For they are the foundation of all business deals.

Be clear, concise, and articulate,

And you'll avoid misunderstandings and debate.

Verse 7:

Embrace diversity and inclusivity,

For a team with different perspectives is key.

Respect and appreciate all backgrounds and opinions,

And you'll foster a culture of collaboration.

Verse 8:

Learn from your failures and setbacks,

For they are opportunities to grow and adapt.

Reflect on what went wrong and how to improve,

And you'll turn failure into success, that's the groove.

Verse 9:

Stay up-to-date on the latest trends and technology,

And invest in the tools that will drive your company.

Don't be afraid to experiment and take risks,

And you'll stay ahead of the competition and reap the benefits.

Verse 10:

Lead by example and inspire your team,

For they are the ones who will make your vision a dream.

Show gratitude, kindness, and empathy,

And you'll create a workplace of happiness and synergy.

CHAPTER THIRTY-EIGHT

Below are some websites useful for CTO's

1. Zoho Creator - https://www.zoho.com/creator/
2. Bubble - https://bubble.io/
3. AppSheet - https://www.appsheet.com/
4. Mendix - https://www.mendix.com/
5. OutSystems - https://www.outsystems.com/
6. Codeless Platforms - https://www.codelessplatforms.com/
7. Appian - https://www.appian.com/
8. Betty Blocks - https://www.bettyblocks.com/
9. WaveMaker - https://www.wavemaker.com/
10. Appy Pie - https://www.appypie.com/
11. Quick Base - https://www.quickbase.com/
12. Kissflow - https://kissflow.com/
13. Joget Workflow - https://www.joget.org/
14. Caspio - https://www.caspio.com/
15. Progress Rollbase - https://www.progress.com/rollbase

16. Microsoft Power Apps - https://powerapps.microsoft.com/
17. Kintone - https://www.kintone.com/
18. FileMaker - https://www.filemaker.com/
19. AppFusion - https://www.appfusion.com/
20. AgilePoint NX - https://agilepoint.com/
21. Alpha Anywhere - https://www.alphasoftware.com/
22. Appian - https://www.appian.com/
23. AppSheet - https://www.appsheet.com/
24. Appy Pie - https://www.appypie.com/
25. Axway Appcelerator - https://www.axway.com/en/appcelerator
26. Betty Blocks - https://www.bettyblocks.com/
27. Bizness Apps - https://www.biznessapps.com/
28. BuildFire - https://buildfire.com/
29. Codeless Platforms - https://www.codelessplatforms.com/
30. Corvid by Wix - https://www.wix.com/corvid
31. Crowd Machine - https://www.crowdmachine.com/
32. FileMaker - https://www.filemaker.com/
33. Google App Maker - https://developers.google.com/appmaker/
34. Indigo.Design - https://www.infragistics.com/products/indigo-design
35. Intellimas - https://www.intellimas.com/
36. Joget Workflow - https://www.joget.org/
37. Kintone - https://www.kintone.com/
38. Kony Quantum - https://www.kony.com/products/quantum
39. Low-Code Studio - https://www.low-code-studio.com/
40. Magic - https://www.magicsoftware.com/
41. Mendix - https://www.mendix.com/

42. Microsoft Power Apps - https://powerapps.microsoft.com/
43. Neonto Studio - https://www.neonto.com/
44. NoCodeAPI - https://nocodeapi.com/
45. OutSystems - https://www.outsystems.com/
46. Quick Base - https://www.quickbase.com/
47. Quixy - https://quixy.com/
48. Salesforce Lightning Platform - https://www.salesforce.com/products/platform/overview/
49. Scopeland Technology - https://www.scopelandtechnology.com/
50. ServiceNow - https://www.servicenow.com/
51. Simplifier - https://simplifier.io/
52. SmartBear HipTest - https://www.hiptest.com/
53. Snappii - https://www.snappii.com/
54. Sodadb - https://www.sodadb.com/
55. Springbuilder - https://springbuilder.net/
56. TARA - https://tara.ai/
57. OpenAI (https://openai.com/)
58. TensorFlow (https://www.tensorflow.org/)
59. Keras (https://keras.io/)
60. PyTorch (https://pytorch.org/)
61. Caffe (http://caffe.berkeleyvision.org/)
62. Microsoft Azure (https://azure.microsoft.com/en-us/overview/ai-platform/)
63. Google Cloud AI Platform (https://cloud.google.com/ai-platform/)
64. IBM Watson Studio (https://www.ibm.com/cloud/watson-studio)
65. Amazon SageMaker (https://aws.amazon.com/sagemaker/)
66. DataRobot (https://www.datarobot.com/)

67. H2O.ai (https://www.h2o.ai/)
68. Algorithmia (https://algorithmia.com/)
69. NVIDIA Deep Learning Institute (https://www.nvidia.com/en-us/deep-learning-ai/education/)
70. MLflow (https://mlflow.org/)
71. AccuRate (https://accu-rate.ca/)
72. Appen (https://appen.com/)
73. Big Panda (https://www.bigpanda.io/)
74. Bitnami (https://bitnami.com/)
75. Blue River Technology (https://www.bluerivertechnology.com/)
76. CloudFactory (https://www.cloudfactory.com/)
77. CloudMinds (https://www.cloudminds.com/)
78. CloudFactory (https://www.cloudfactory.com/)
79. CrowdFlower (https://www.crowdflower.com/)
80. Cognitivescale (https://cognitivescale.com/)
81. Databricks (https://databricks.com/)
82. Dataturks (https://dataturks.com/)
83. Deepgram (https://deepgram.com/)
84. DeepScale (https://deepscale.ai/)
85. Dataiku (https://www.dataiku.com/)
86. Edgecase (https://www.edgecase.ai/)
87. Freenome (https://www.freenome.com/)
88. Gamalon (https://www.gamalon.com/)
89. Gradient (https://gradient.paperspace.com/)
90. HyperScience (https://hyperscience.com/)
91. Indico Data Solutions (https://indico.io/)
92. Infosys Nia (https://www.infosys.com/ai-automation/nia/)
93. Intel Nervana AI Academy (https://www.intelnervana.com/academia/)
94. KAI (https://www.kai.ai/)

95. Luminoso (https://luminoso.com/)
96. Machine Learning Mastery (https://machinelearningmastery.com/)
97. Mad Street Den (https://madstreetden.com/)
98. MindMeld (https://www.mindmeld.com/)
99. Neurala (https://www.neurala.com/)
100. Nexosis (https://www.nexosis.com/)
101. ParallelDots (https://www.paralleldots.com/)
102. Playment (https://playment.io/)
103. RapidMiner (https://rapidminer.com/)
104. Receptiviti (https://receptiviti.com/)
105. Suki.AI (https://suki.ai/)
106. Vicarious (https://www.vicarious.com/)

Thank you for taking the time to read this book thereby making your business a success. We hope that the insights and strategies presented here have been helpful in your journey towards creating smarter, more efficient, and more effective organizations.

As a CTO, you play a crucial role in the technological development of your company. By leveraging AI and other cutting-edge technologies, you can create innovative products and services that drive growth and success.

As a CEO, you have a vision for your company and the responsibility to make that vision a reality. By understanding how to use AI to your advantage, you can make more informed decisions and lead your company to greater success.

As a CMO, your goal is to effectively communicate your company's message and generate leads. By incorporating AI into your marketing strategies, you can personalize your outreach and increase your chances of reaching the right people at the right time.

And as a freelancer, you have the opportunity to leverage AI to increase your productivity and effectiveness. By embracing new tools and technologies, you can provide more value to your clients and stand out in a crowded marketplace.

We wish you all the best in your future endeavors, and hope that this book has been a valuable resource in your quest for business success.

I am available to you face-to-face as an AI 24x7 to answer all your queries in less than 5 minutes. All you have to do is scan the QR code, register, login, and type your question in the text box.

9 798890 023186

Printed by Libri Plureos GmbH in Hamburg, Germany